Keep Track of Your Food!
A Monthly Meal Planner

Copyright 2016

All Rights reserved. No part of this book may be reproduced or used in any way or formor by any means whether electronic or mechanical, this means that you cannot recordor photocopy any material ideas or tips that are provided in this book.

Keep Track of Your Food! A Monthly Meal Planner

Name: Month:

	Monday	Tuesday	Wednesday
Breakfast			
Snack			
Lunch			
Snack			
Dinner			
Snack			

Recipes: Groceries   Notes:

Vitamins   Drinks   Notes:

Keep Track of Your Food! A Monthly Meal Planner

Name: Month:

	Monday	Tuesday	Wednesday
Breakfast			
Snack			
Lunch			
Snack			
Dinner			
Snack			

Recipes: Groceries   Notes:

Vitamins   Drinks   Notes:

Keep Track of Your Food! A Monthly Meal Planner

Name: Month:

	Monday	Tuesday	Wednesday
Breakfast			
Snack			
Lunch			
Snack			
Dinner			
Snack			

Recipes: Groceries Notes:

Vitamins Drinks Notes:

Keep Track of Your Food! A Monthly Meal Planner

Name: Month:

	Monday	Tuesday	Wednesday
Breakfast			
Snack			
Lunch			
Snack			
Dinner			
Snack			

Recipes: Groceries   Notes:

Vitamins   Drinks   Notes:

Keep Track of Your Food! A Monthly Meal Planner

Name: Month:

	Monday	Tuesday	Wednesday
Breakfast			
Snack			
Lunch			
Snack			
Dinner			
Snack			

Recipes: Groceries   Notes:

Vitamins   Drinks   Notes:

Keep Track of Your Food! A Monthly Meal Planner

Name: Month:

	Monday	Tuesday	Wednesday
Breakfast			
Snack			
Lunch			
Snack			
Dinner			
Snack			

Recipes: Groceries   Notes:

Vitamins   Drinks   Notes:

Keep Track of Your Food! A Monthly Meal Planner

Name: Month:

	Monday	Tuesday	Wednesday
Breakfast			
Snack			
Lunch			
Snack			
Dinner			
Snack			

Recipes: Groceries   Notes:

Vitamins   Drinks   Notes:

Keep Track of Your Food! A Monthly Meal Planner

Name: Month:

	Monday	Tuesday	Wednesday
Breakfast			
Snack			
Lunch			
Snack			
Dinner			
Snack			

Recipes: Groceries   Notes:

Vitamins   Drinks   Notes:

Keep Track of Your Food! A Monthly Meal Planner

Name: Month:

	Monday	Tuesday	Wednesday
Breakfast			
Snack			
Lunch			
Snack			
Dinner			
Snack			

Recipes: Groceries   Notes:

Vitamins   Drinks   Notes:

Keep Track of Your Food! A Monthly Meal Planner

Name: Month:

	Monday	Tuesday	Wednesday
Breakfast			
Snack			
Lunch			
Snack			
Dinner			
Snack			

Recipes: Groceries   Notes:

Vitamins   Drinks   Notes:

Keep Track of Your Food! A Monthly Meal Planner

Name: Month:

	Monday	Tuesday	Wednesday
Breakfast			
Snack			
Lunch			
Snack			
Dinner			
Snack			

Recipes: Groceries Notes:

Vitamins Drinks Notes:

Keep Track of Your Food! A Monthly Meal Planner

Name: Month:

	Monday	Tuesday	Wednesday
Breakfast			
Snack			
Lunch			
Snack			
Dinner			
Snack			

Recipes: Groceries   Notes:

Vitamins   Drinks   Notes:

Keep Track of Your Food! A Monthly Meal Planner

Name: Month:

	Monday	Tuesday	Wednesday
Breakfast			
Snack			
Lunch			
Snack			
Dinner			
Snack			

Recipes: Groceries   Notes:

Vitamins   Drinks   Notes:

Keep Track of Your Food! A Monthly Meal Planner

Name: Month:

	Monday	Tuesday	Wednesday
Breakfast			
Snack			
Lunch			
Snack			
Dinner			
Snack			

Recipes: Groceries   Notes:

Vitamins   Drinks   Notes:

Keep Track of Your Food! A Monthly Meal Planner

Name: Month:

	Monday	Tuesday	Wednesday
Breakfast			
Snack			
Lunch			
Snack			
Dinner			
Snack			

Recipes: Groceries   Notes:

Vitamins   Drinks   Notes:

Keep Track of Your Food! A Monthly Meal Planner

Name: Month:

	Monday	Tuesday	Wednesday
Breakfast			
Snack			
Lunch			
Snack			
Dinner			
Snack			

Recipes: Groceries   Notes:

Vitamins   Drinks   Notes:

Keep Track of Your Food! A Monthly Meal Planner

Name: Month:

	Monday	Tuesday	Wednesday
Breakfast			
Snack			
Lunch			
Snack			
Dinner			
Snack			

Recipes: Groceries   Notes:

Vitamins   Drinks   Notes:

Keep Track of Your Food! A Monthly Meal Planner

Name: Month:

	Monday	Tuesday	Wednesday
Breakfast			
Snack			
Lunch			
Snack			
Dinner			
Snack			

Recipes: Groceries   Notes:

Vitamins   Drinks   Notes:

Keep Track of Your Food! A Monthly Meal Planner

Name: Month:

	Monday	Tuesday	Wednesday
Breakfast			
Snack			
Lunch			
Snack			
Dinner			
Snack			

Recipes: Groceries   Notes:

Vitamins   Drinks   Notes:

Keep Track of Your Food! A Monthly Meal Planner

Name: Month:

	Monday	Tuesday	Wednesday
Breakfast			
Snack			
Lunch			
Snack			
Dinner			
Snack			

Recipes: Groceries   Notes:

Vitamins   Drinks   Notes:

Keep Track of Your Food! A Monthly Meal Planner

Name: Month:

	Monday	Tuesday	Wednesday
Breakfast			
Snack			
Lunch			
Snack			
Dinner			
Snack			

Recipes: Groceries Notes:

Vitamins Drinks Notes:

Keep Track of Your Food! A Monthly Meal Planner

Name: Month:

	Monday	Tuesday	Wednesday
Breakfast			
Snack			
Lunch			
Snack			
Dinner			
Snack			

Recipes: Groceries Notes:

Vitamins Drinks Notes:

Keep Track of Your Food! A Monthly Meal Planner

Name: Month:

	Monday	Tuesday	Wednesday
Breakfast			
Snack			
Lunch			
Snack			
Dinner			
Snack			

Recipes: Groceries   Notes:

Vitamins   Drinks   Notes:

Keep Track of Your Food! A Monthly Meal Planner

Name: Month:

	Monday	Tuesday	Wednesday
Breakfast			
Snack			
Lunch			
Snack			
Dinner			
Snack			

Recipes: Groceries   Notes:

Vitamins   Drinks   Notes:

Keep Track of Your Food! A Monthly Meal Planner

Name: Month:

	Monday	Tuesday	Wednesday
Breakfast			
Snack			
Lunch			
Snack			
Dinner			
Snack			

Recipes: Groceries Notes:

Vitamins Drinks Notes:

Keep Track of Your Food! A Monthly Meal Planner

Name: Month:

	Monday	Tuesday	Wednesday
Breakfast			
Snack			
Lunch			
Snack			
Dinner			
Snack			

Recipes: Groceries   Notes:

Vitamins   Drinks   Notes:

Keep Track of Your Food! A Monthly Meal Planner

Name: Month:

	Monday	Tuesday	Wednesday
Breakfast			
Snack			
Lunch			
Snack			
Dinner			
Snack			

Recipes: Groceries   Notes:

Vitamins   Drinks   Notes:

Keep Track of Your Food! A Monthly Meal Planner

Name: Month:

	Monday	Tuesday	Wednesday
Breakfast			
Snack			
Lunch			
Snack			
Dinner			
Snack			

Recipes: Groceries   Notes:

Vitamins   Drinks   Notes:

Keep Track of Your Food! A Monthly Meal Planner

Name: Month:

	Monday	Tuesday	Wednesday
Breakfast			
Snack			
Lunch			
Snack			
Dinner			
Snack			

Recipes: Groceries   Notes:

Vitamins   Drinks   Notes:

Keep Track of Your Food! A Monthly Meal Planner

Name: Month:

	Monday	Tuesday	Wednesday
Breakfast			
Snack			
Lunch			
Snack			
Dinner			
Snack			

Recipes: Groceries   Notes:

Vitamins   Drinks   Notes:

	Keep Track of Your Food! A Monthly Meal Planner		
Name:			Month:

	Monday	Tuesday	Wednesday
Breakfast			
Snack			
Lunch			
Snack			
Dinner			
Snack			

Recipes:	Groceries	Notes:

Vitamins	Drinks	Notes:

Keep Track of Your Food! A Monthly Meal Planner

Name: Month:

	Monday	Tuesday	Wednesday
Breakfast			
Snack			
Lunch			
Snack			
Dinner			
Snack			

Recipes: Groceries   Notes:

Vitamins   Drinks   Notes:

Keep Track of Your Food! A Monthly Meal Planner

Name: Month:

	Monday	Tuesday	Wednesday
Breakfast			
Snack			
Lunch			
Snack			
Dinner			
Snack			

Recipes: Groceries Notes:

Vitamins Drinks Notes:

Keep Track of Your Food! A Monthly Meal Planner

Name: Month:

	Monday	Tuesday	Wednesday
Breakfast			
Snack			
Lunch			
Snack			
Dinner			
Snack			

Recipes: Groceries   Notes:

Vitamins   Drinks   Notes:

Keep Track of Your Food! A Monthly Meal Planner

Name: Month:

	Monday	Tuesday	Wednesday
Breakfast			
Snack			
Lunch			
Snack			
Dinner			
Snack			

Recipes: Groceries   Notes:

Vitamins   Drinks   Notes:

Keep Track of Your Food! A Monthly Meal Planner

Name: Month:

	Monday	Tuesday	Wednesday
Breakfast			
Snack			
Lunch			
Snack			
Dinner			
Snack			

Recipes: Groceries Notes:

Vitamins Drinks Notes:

Keep Track of Your Food! A Monthly Meal Planner

Name: Month:

	Monday	Tuesday	Wednesday
Breakfast			
Snack			
Lunch			
Snack			
Dinner			
Snack			

Recipes: Groceries   Notes:

Vitamins   Drinks   Notes:

Keep Track of Your Food! A Monthly Meal Planner

Name: Month:

	Monday	Tuesday	Wednesday
Breakfast			
Snack			
Lunch			
Snack			
Dinner			
Snack			

Recipes: Groceries Notes:

Vitamins Drinks Notes:

Keep Track of Your Food! A Monthly Meal Planner

Name: Month:

	Monday	Tuesday	Wednesday
Breakfast			
Snack			
Lunch			
Snack			
Dinner			
Snack			

Recipes: Groceries   Notes:

Vitamins   Drinks   Notes:

Keep Track of Your Food! A Monthly Meal Planner

Name: Month:

	Monday	Tuesday	Wednesday
Breakfast			
Snack			
Lunch			
Snack			
Dinner			
Snack			

Recipes: Groceries   Notes:

Vitamins   Drinks   Notes:

Keep Track of Your Food! A Monthly Meal Planner

Name: Month:

	Monday	Tuesday	Wednesday
Breakfast			
Snack			
Lunch			
Snack			
Dinner			
Snack			

Recipes: Groceries   Notes:

Vitamins   Drinks   Notes:

Keep Track of Your Food! A Monthly Meal Planner

Name: Month:

	Monday	Tuesday	Wednesday
Breakfast			
Snack			
Lunch			
Snack			
Dinner			
Snack			

Recipes: Groceries   Notes:

Vitamins   Drinks   Notes:

Keep Track of Your Food! A Monthly Meal Planner

Name: Month:

	Monday	Tuesday	Wednesday
Breakfast			
Snack			
Lunch			
Snack			
Dinner			
Snack			

Recipes: Groceries   Notes:

Vitamins   Drinks   Notes:

Keep Track of Your Food! A Monthly Meal Planner

Name: Month:

	Monday	Tuesday	Wednesday
Breakfast			
Snack			
Lunch			
Snack			
Dinner			
Snack			

Recipes: Groceries Notes:

Vitamins Drinks Notes:

Keep Track of Your Food! A Monthly Meal Planner

Name: Month:

	Monday	Tuesday	Wednesday
Breakfast			
Snack			
Lunch			
Snack			
Dinner			
Snack			

Recipes: Groceries   Notes:

Vitamins   Drinks   Notes:

Keep Track of Your Food! A Monthly Meal Planner

Name: Month:

	Monday	Tuesday	Wednesday
Breakfast			
Snack			
Lunch			
Snack			
Dinner			
Snack			

Recipes: Groceries   Notes:

Vitamins   Drinks   Notes:

Keep Track of Your Food! A Monthly Meal Planner

Name: Month:

	Monday	Tuesday	Wednesday
Breakfast			
Snack			
Lunch			
Snack			
Dinner			
Snack			

Recipes: Groceries   Notes:

Vitamins   Drinks   Notes:

Keep Track of Your Food! A Monthly Meal Planner

Name: Month:

	Monday	Tuesday	Wednesday
Breakfast			
Snack			
Lunch			
Snack			
Dinner			
Snack			

Recipes: Groceries   Notes:

Vitamins   Drinks   Notes:

Keep Track of Your Food! A Monthly Meal Planner

Name: _____ Month: _____

	Monday	Tuesday	Wednesday
Breakfast			
Snack			
Lunch			
Snack			
Dinner			
Snack			

Recipes: Groceries   Notes:

Vitamins   Drinks   Notes:

Keep Track of Your Food! A Monthly Meal Planner

Name: Month:

	Monday	Tuesday	Wednesday
Breakfast			
Snack			
Lunch			
Snack			
Dinner			
Snack			

Recipes: Groceries   Notes:

Vitamins   Drinks   Notes:

Keep Track of Your Food! A Monthly Meal Planner

Name: Month:

	Monday	Tuesday	Wednesday
Breakfast			
Snack			
Lunch			
Snack			
Dinner			
Snack			

Recipes: Groceries Notes:

Vitamins Drinks Notes:

Keep Track of Your Food! A Monthly Meal Planner

Name: Month:

	Monday	Tuesday	Wednesday
Breakfast			
Snack			
Lunch			
Snack			
Dinner			
Snack			

Recipes: Groceries   Notes:

Vitamins   Drinks   Notes:

Keep Track of Your Food! A Monthly Meal Planner

Name: Month:

	Monday	Tuesday	Wednesday
Breakfast			
Snack			
Lunch			
Snack			
Dinner			
Snack			

Recipes: Groceries   Notes:

Vitamins   Drinks   Notes:

Keep Track of Your Food! A Monthly Meal Planner

Name: Month:

	Monday	Tuesday	Wednesday
Breakfast			
Snack			
Lunch			
Snack			
Dinner			
Snack			

Recipes: Groceries   Notes:

Vitamins   Drinks   Notes:

Keep Track of Your Food! A Monthly Meal Planner

Name: Month:

	Monday	Tuesday	Wednesday
Breakfast			
Snack			
Lunch			
Snack			
Dinner			
Snack			

Recipes: Groceries   Notes:

Vitamins   Drinks   Notes:

Keep Track of Your Food! A Monthly Meal Planner

Name: Month:

	Monday	Tuesday	Wednesday
Breakfast			
Snack			
Lunch			
Snack			
Dinner			
Snack			

Recipes: Groceries   Notes:

Vitamins   Drinks   Notes:

Keep Track of Your Food! A Monthly Meal Planner

Name: Month:

	Monday	Tuesday	Wednesday
Breakfast			
Snack			
Lunch			
Snack			
Dinner			
Snack			

Recipes: Groceries   Notes:

Vitamins   Drinks   Notes:

Keep Track of Your Food! A Monthly Meal Planner

Name: Month:

	Monday	Tuesday	Wednesday
Breakfast			
Snack			
Lunch			
Snack			
Dinner			
Snack			

Recipes: Groceries   Notes:

Vitamins   Drinks   Notes:

Keep Track of Your Food! A Monthly Meal Planner

Name: Month:

	Monday	Tuesday	Wednesday
Breakfast			
Snack			
Lunch			
Snack			
Dinner			
Snack			

Recipes: Groceries Notes:

Vitamins Drinks Notes:

Keep Track of Your Food! A Monthly Meal Planner

Name: Month:

	Monday	Tuesday	Wednesday
Breakfast			
Snack			
Lunch			
Snack			
Dinner			
Snack			

Recipes: Groceries   Notes:

Vitamins   Drinks   Notes:

Keep Track of Your Food! A Monthly Meal Planner

Name: Month:

	Monday	Tuesday	Wednesday
Breakfast			
Snack			
Lunch			
Snack			
Dinner			
Snack			

Recipes: Groceries   Notes:

Vitamins   Drinks   Notes:

Keep Track of Your Food! A Monthly Meal Planner

Name: Month:

	Monday	Tuesday	Wednesday
Breakfast			
Snack			
Lunch			
Snack			
Dinner			
Snack			

Recipes: Groceries   Notes:

Vitamins   Drinks   Notes:

Keep Track of Your Food! A Monthly Meal Planner

Name:　　　　　　　　　　　　　　　　　　　　　　　Month:

	Monday	Tuesday	Wednesday
Breakfast			
Snack			
Lunch			
Snack			
Dinner			
Snack			

Recipes:　　　　　　　　　Groceries　　　　　　　　　Notes:

Vitamins　　　　　　　　　Drinks　　　　　　　　　　Notes:

Keep Track of Your Food! A Monthly Meal Planner

Name: Month:

	Monday	Tuesday	Wednesday
Breakfast			
Snack			
Lunch			
Snack			
Dinner			
Snack			

Recipes: Groceries Notes:

Vitamins Drinks Notes:

Keep Track of Your Food! A Monthly Meal Planner

Name: Month:

	Monday	Tuesday	Wednesday
Breakfast			
Snack			
Lunch			
Snack			
Dinner			
Snack			

Recipes: Groceries Notes:

Vitamins Drinks Notes:

Keep Track of Your Food! A Monthly Meal Planner

Name: Month:

	Monday	Tuesday	Wednesday
Breakfast			
Snack			
Lunch			
Snack			
Dinner			
Snack			

Recipes: Groceries   Notes:

Vitamins   Drinks   Notes:

Keep Track of Your Food! A Monthly Meal Planner

Name: Month:

	Monday	Tuesday	Wednesday
Breakfast			
Snack			
Lunch			
Snack			
Dinner			
Snack			

Recipes: Groceries   Notes:

Vitamins   Drinks   Notes:

Keep Track of Your Food! A Monthly Meal Planner

Name: Month:

	Monday	Tuesday	Wednesday
Breakfast			
Snack			
Lunch			
Snack			
Dinner			
Snack			

Recipes: Groceries   Notes:

Vitamins   Drinks   Notes:

Keep Track of Your Food! A Monthly Meal Planner

Name: Month:

	Monday	Tuesday	Wednesday
Breakfast			
Snack			
Lunch			
Snack			
Dinner			
Snack			

Recipes: Groceries   Notes:

Vitamins   Drinks   Notes:

Keep Track of Your Food! A Monthly Meal Planner

Name: Month:

	Monday	Tuesday	Wednesday
Breakfast			
Snack			
Lunch			
Snack			
Dinner			
Snack			

Recipes: Groceries   Notes:

Vitamins   Drinks   Notes:

Keep Track of Your Food! A Monthly Meal Planner

Name: Month:

	Monday	Tuesday	Wednesday
Breakfast			
Snack			
Lunch			
Snack			
Dinner			
Snack			

Recipes: Groceries   Notes:

Vitamins   Drinks   Notes:

Keep Track of Your Food! A Monthly Meal Planner

Name: Month:

	Monday	Tuesday	Wednesday
Breakfast			
Snack			
Lunch			
Snack			
Dinner			
Snack			

Recipes: Groceries Notes:

Vitamins Drinks Notes:

Keep Track of Your Food! A Monthly Meal Planner

Name: Month:

	Monday	Tuesday	Wednesday
Breakfast			
Snack			
Lunch			
Snack			
Dinner			
Snack			

Recipes: Groceries Notes:

Vitamins Drinks Notes:

Keep Track of Your Food! A Monthly Meal Planner

Name: Month:

	Monday	Tuesday	Wednesday
Breakfast			
Snack			
Lunch			
Snack			
Dinner			
Snack			

Recipes: Groceries   Notes:

Vitamins   Drinks   Notes:

Keep Track of Your Food! A Monthly Meal Planner

Name: Month:

	Monday	Tuesday	Wednesday
Breakfast			
Snack			
Lunch			
Snack			
Dinner			
Snack			

Recipes: Groceries   Notes:

Vitamins   Drinks   Notes:

Keep Track of Your Food! A Monthly Meal Planner

Name: Month:

	Monday	Tuesday	Wednesday
Breakfast			
Snack			
Lunch			
Snack			
Dinner			
Snack			

Recipes: Groceries   Notes:

Vitamins   Drinks   Notes:

Keep Track of Your Food! A Monthly Meal Planner

Name: Month:

	Monday	Tuesday	Wednesday
Breakfast			
Snack			
Lunch			
Snack			
Dinner			
Snack			

Recipes: Groceries   Notes:

Vitamins   Drinks   Notes:

Keep Track of Your Food! A Monthly Meal Planner

Name: Month:

	Monday	Tuesday	Wednesday
Breakfast			
Snack			
Lunch			
Snack			
Dinner			
Snack			

Recipes: Groceries   Notes:

Vitamins   Drinks   Notes:

Keep Track of Your Food! A Monthly Meal Planner

Name: Month:

	Monday	Tuesday	Wednesday
Breakfast			
Snack			
Lunch			
Snack			
Dinner			
Snack			

Recipes: Groceries   Notes:

Vitamins   Drinks   Notes:

Keep Track of Your Food! A Monthly Meal Planner

Name: Month:

	Monday	Tuesday	Wednesday
Breakfast			
Snack			
Lunch			
Snack			
Dinner			
Snack			

Recipes: Groceries   Notes:

Vitamins   Drinks   Notes:

Keep Track of Your Food! A Monthly Meal Planner

Name: Month:

	Monday	Tuesday	Wednesday
Breakfast			
Snack			
Lunch			
Snack			
Dinner			
Snack			

Recipes: Groceries   Notes:

Vitamins   Drinks   Notes:

Keep Track of Your Food! A Monthly Meal Planner

Name: Month:

	Monday	Tuesday	Wednesday
Breakfast			
Snack			
Lunch			
Snack			
Dinner			
Snack			

Recipes: Groceries   Notes:

Vitamins   Drinks   Notes:

Keep Track of Your Food! A Monthly Meal Planner

Name: Month:

	Monday	Tuesday	Wednesday
Breakfast			
Snack			
Lunch			
Snack			
Dinner			
Snack			

Recipes: Groceries Notes:

Vitamins Drinks Notes:

Keep Track of Your Food! A Monthly Meal Planner

Name: Month:

	Monday	Tuesday	Wednesday
Breakfast			
Snack			
Lunch			
Snack			
Dinner			
Snack			

Recipes: Groceries   Notes:

Vitamins   Drinks   Notes:

Keep Track of Your Food! A Monthly Meal Planner

Name: Month:

	Monday	Tuesday	Wednesday
Breakfast			
Snack			
Lunch			
Snack			
Dinner			
Snack			

Recipes: Groceries Notes:

Vitamins Drinks Notes:

Keep Track of Your Food! A Monthly Meal Planner

Name: Month:

	Monday	Tuesday	Wednesday
Breakfast			
Snack			
Lunch			
Snack			
Dinner			
Snack			

Recipes: Groceries   Notes:

Vitamins   Drinks   Notes:

Keep Track of Your Food! A Monthly Meal Planner

Name: Month:

	Monday	Tuesday	Wednesday
Breakfast			
Snack			
Lunch			
Snack			
Dinner			
Snack			

Recipes: Groceries   Notes:

Vitamins   Drinks   Notes:

Keep Track of Your Food! A Monthly Meal Planner

Name: Month:

	Monday	Tuesday	Wednesday
Breakfast			
Snack			
Lunch			
Snack			
Dinner			
Snack			

Recipes: Groceries   Notes:

Vitamins   Drinks   Notes:

Keep Track of Your Food! A Monthly Meal Planner

Name: Month:

	Monday	Tuesday	Wednesday
Breakfast			
Snack			
Lunch			
Snack			
Dinner			
Snack			

Recipes: Groceries   Notes:

Vitamins   Drinks   Notes:

Keep Track of Your Food! A Monthly Meal Planner

Name: Month:

	Monday	Tuesday	Wednesday
Breakfast			
Snack			
Lunch			
Snack			
Dinner			
Snack			

Recipes: Groceries   Notes:

Vitamins   Drinks   Notes:

Keep Track of Your Food! A Monthly Meal Planner

Name: Month:

	Monday	Tuesday	Wednesday
Breakfast			
Snack			
Lunch			
Snack			
Dinner			
Snack			

Recipes: Groceries   Notes:

Vitamins   Drinks   Notes:

Keep Track of Your Food! A Monthly Meal Planner

Name: Month:

	Monday	Tuesday	Wednesday
Breakfast			
Snack			
Lunch			
Snack			
Dinner			
Snack			

Recipes: Groceries   Notes:

Vitamins   Drinks   Notes:

Keep Track of Your Food! A Monthly Meal Planner

Name: Month:

	Monday	Tuesday	Wednesday
Breakfast			
Snack			
Lunch			
Snack			
Dinner			
Snack			

Recipes: Groceries Notes:

Vitamins Drinks Notes:

Keep Track of Your Food! A Monthly Meal Planner

Name: Month:

	Monday	Tuesday	Wednesday
Breakfast			
Snack			
Lunch			
Snack			
Dinner			
Snack			

Recipes: Groceries   Notes:

Vitamins   Drinks   Notes:

Keep Track of Your Food! A Monthly Meal Planner

Name: Month:

	Monday	Tuesday	Wednesday
Breakfast			
Snack			
Lunch			
Snack			
Dinner			
Snack			

Recipes: Groceries   Notes:

Vitamins   Drinks   Notes:

Keep Track of Your Food! A Monthly Meal Planner

Name: Month:

	Monday	Tuesday	Wednesday
Breakfast			
Snack			
Lunch			
Snack			
Dinner			
Snack			

Recipes: Groceries Notes:

Vitamins Drinks Notes:

Keep Track of Your Food! A Monthly Meal Planner

Name: _____   Month: _____

	Monday	Tuesday	Wednesday
Breakfast			
Snack			
Lunch			
Snack			
Dinner			
Snack			

Recipes: Groceries   Notes:

Vitamins   Drinks   Notes:

Keep Track of Your Food! A Monthly Meal Planner

Name: Month:

	Monday	Tuesday	Wednesday
Breakfast			
Snack			
Lunch			
Snack			
Dinner			
Snack			

Recipes: Groceries   Notes:

Vitamins   Drinks   Notes:

Keep Track of Your Food! A Monthly Meal Planner

Name: Month:

	Monday	Tuesday	Wednesday
Breakfast			
Snack			
Lunch			
Snack			
Dinner			
Snack			

Recipes: Groceries   Notes:

Vitamins   Drinks   Notes:

Keep Track of Your Food! A Monthly Meal Planner

Name: Month:

	Monday	Tuesday	Wednesday
Breakfast			
Snack			
Lunch			
Snack			
Dinner			
Snack			

Recipes: Groceries   Notes:

Vitamins   Drinks   Notes:

Keep Track of Your Food! A Monthly Meal Planner

Name: Month:

	Monday	Tuesday	Wednesday
Breakfast			
Snack			
Lunch			
Snack			
Dinner			
Snack			

Recipes: Groceries   Notes:

Vitamins   Drinks   Notes:

Keep Track of Your Food! A Monthly Meal Planner

Name: Month:

	Monday	Tuesday	Wednesday
Breakfast			
Snack			
Lunch			
Snack			
Dinner			
Snack			

Recipes: Groceries   Notes:

Vitamins   Drinks   Notes:

Keep Track of Your Food! A Monthly Meal Planner

Name: Month:

	Monday	Tuesday	Wednesday
Breakfast			
Snack			
Lunch			
Snack			
Dinner			
Snack			

Recipes: Groceries   Notes:

Vitamins   Drinks   Notes:

Keep Track of Your Food! A Monthly Meal Planner

Name: Month:

	Monday	Tuesday	Wednesday
Breakfast			
Snack			
Lunch			
Snack			
Dinner			
Snack			

Recipes: Groceries   Notes:

Vitamins   Drinks   Notes:

www.ingramcontent.com/pod-product-compliance
Lightning Source LLC
LaVergne TN
LVHW081524060526
838200LV00044B/1994